MANY WAYS TO GOD?

5

Five Religious Leaders discover the truth

JOHN RITCHIE LTD
CHRISTIAN PUBLICATIONS

40 Beansburn, Kilmarnock, Scotland

Contents

Introduction

The 20th century witnessed a gradual and increasingly successful effort to unite all the world's religions under one roof. Today the ecumenical movement has become a global phenomenon involving millions of people from all continents. 9/11 and religious extremism in general has given the world a fresh impetus to pursue religious understanding at all costs. Is this to be welcomed or are we sacrificing truth and integrity on the altar of syncretic political correctness?

In this book five religious leaders speak out. Though from totally different backgrounds, a Tibetan Buddhist monk, a Muslim imam, a Jewish rabbi, a Hindu and a Catholic priest all unite around a common faith and hope for the future.

CHAPTER 1

Destined for Royalty
(The Testimony of a Hindu Priest)

Anand Chaudhari
India

Anand Chaudhari descended from a long line of famous Hindu Brahmin priests in Goa, India. His father, Sushi Kumar Chaudhari, who took the title 'Shastri' – one who has mastered the Hindu Scriptures – was the chief priest of the temple called the Shri Santadurga, one of the Kashmiri Brahmins' three most important places of worship in Goa. Sushi Kumar frequently travelled throughout India lecturing leading Hindus on their sacred writings. In 1939 an outbreak of smallpox decimated Goa's population, taking four of Anand's brothers in death. The disease struck Anand himself, an experience that remained vivid in his mind for the rest of his life. In his own words:

"One night my father sat at my bedside and, seeing my life slipping away, from the depths of his heart he prayed to God, a God he did not even know. I remember that prayer. My father promised that if God would spare me, I would be given to Him for His service. He doubtless meant this to be as a Hindu priest, but how differently God answered. He did hear that prayer, and I recovered."

With many millions of different gods worshipped in India, Sushi Kumar's prayer seemed somewhat unusual. Perhaps

4

somewhere in the back of his mind he believed in a supreme deity yet unknown to him. After the death of his four sons, Anand's father sank into deep depression. What terrible sins had he committed in his former life to inflict such a heavy karma? At times the guilt seemed unbearable. What acts of penance could possibly expiate all the evils of his past life? Other than performing the necessary regular priestly functions in the temple, Sushi Kumar withdrew into Yoga, meditation and the endless recitation of mantras, especially the word 'OM' (or 'AUM'), which represents Brahman, the impersonal force of the universe.

Determined not to renege on his promise to God, Sushi Kumar began to train his son Anand in the disciplines of the Hindu priesthood. Under the tutelage of his father and other priests, Anand studied the sacred writings of the Vedas, Upanishads, Bhagavad-Gita and Ramayana. He learnt how to calculate and construct astrological charts, how to practise Yoga and meditation and how to perform priestly rituals, especially those connected with the goddess Durga, the wife of Shiva, the focus of worship in the Shri Santadurga temple.

Anand memorised endless religious instructions and mantras. The mantras he used as a magical force to 'enchain the power of the gods', to cure or cause disease, to act as a preservative or destructive force, and to cause or erase the effects of spirit possession. One mantra, the famous 'gayatri', reads: *"Let us worship the supreme light of the sun, the god of all things, who can so well guide our understanding like an eye suspended in the vault of heaven."*

Some priests recite the gayatri as many as 1,000 or even 5,000 times a day hoping for the remission of their sins, or to gain wealth, health or happiness. Anand's training also featured warnings. One read: *"Remember, O my son, that there is only one God who is the Creator, Lord and source of all things, whom every Brahmin*

5

should worship in secret. But know also that this is a great mystery that must never be revealed to the vulgar and ignorant people. Should you ever reveal it, surely great misfortune will fall upon you."

His father intended for Anand to gain a good all-round education to further facilitate his priestly calling, so in 1942 he sent him to Bombay (Mumbai) where he stayed with his wealthy uncle and aunt. Throughout his time at school and later at university he never ceased performing his priestly duties. Anand's life was nothing if not busy. At Bombay University Anand took a degree course in philosophy. At the time it was fashionable for students to join the growing Communist movement and, seeing no serious contradiction between the priesthood and a communistic political outlook, Anand signed up. His local Communist organization asked him to run classes for the labouring people in a slum area of Bombay. The experience raised disturbing questions in Anand's mind.

"I visited where the labourers lived. I saw their squalid conditions, fifteen or sixteen people living in a one room shack. There was no running water, no sanitation facilities. The people who had jobs worked like animals for a few cents a day. Hinduism seemed to be always looking back. All you have in this life is a result of fulfilling your karma – what you have done in your past life – and whatever you are doing now will determine your next birth. The Harijan (outcaste) does what he is expected to do, and the Brahmin does what is predestined for him."

As a priest, Anand enjoyed the respect of his local community which frequently called upon him to offer special pujas (ritual sacrifices), to officiate at weddings and cremations and to appease the gods in times of trouble. Privately however, he was becoming increasingly uneasy with the entire belief system of Hinduism. He began to feel that its structure had been deliberately designed to favour and safeguard the rights and privileges of the minority Brahmin ruling class. At the opposite end of the unjust caste system were the hopelessly enfeebled and unfortunate majority, whose belief in reincarnation kept them quiet with the hope of future betterment if they submitted to the religious order and lived good lives. Later Anand reflected:

"What was the purpose of their endless sacrifices and daily rituals? The gods simply locked them into their wretchedness, to live their miserable existence without complaint – to suffer pain to its numbness, to give something out of their nothing, to appease the gods' anger so that perchance they would return in the next life as a man rather than a woman, or a farmer rather than a barber?"

Even Anand's political fervour began to wane. For three years he had readily devoured anything communistic. He had even spoken at Communist rallies. Yet his heart ached with a feeling of emptiness. Disillusionment overwhelmed him as he read the works of several ex-Communists. Then came a turning point.

One night in 1953, the Bombay Communist Party asked Anand to speak at a student debate. His pro-Communist speech drew enthusiastic applause from the audience but when his opponent, a student called Joseph, rose to reply, Anand was in for a shock. Joseph's final words were: *"According to my faith, peace will come in this world only when Jesus Christ comes back to establish His kingdom on earth – and not until then."*

Anand was aghast. Jesus Christ? What could that Western god have to do with peace on earth, never mind providing solutions to the pain and poverty of India? Yet Joseph's statement refused to go away. It constantly played on Anand's mind.

"I tried to forget what I had heard, but I couldn't. That name seemed to be hooked into my mind and I could not shake it loose. Then it struck me.

I had studied just about everything else; why not see what this was all about? So about ten days after the debate I contacted Joseph to find out where I could read more about Jesus Christ."

When the two students met Anand found that Joseph could not fully answer all his questions.

"Read the Bible, especially the Gospels," Joseph said, *"God will talk to you and show you the truth."*

Anand took up the challenge. His thoughtful examination of the words of Jesus left him feeling overawed by the power, majesty and love contained in them. Nothing he recalled in the Hindu religion came close to the teachings of Christ.

"I read through Matthew and the other Gospels," says Anand, *"Much I didn't understand, but I was like parched ground soaking up life-giving water."*

For months he agonised over the gospels, struck by the purity he found in Christ in stark contrast to the immoral and capricious gods of his own religion. He remembered the god Shiva who in a fit of jealousy killed his own son Ganesha by decapitation and replaced his head with the head of an elephant; and the goddess Kali who drinks human blood and wears a necklace of human skulls. As he compared the Hindu gods with Jesus Christ he began to entertain the possibility that Jesus might actually be the true God after all. Yet he also entertained another possibility – what if, as some of the Gurus like Ramakrishna had said, Kali, Rama, Hanuman, Jesus and all the gods, are all able to lead to enlightenment? Yet the more Anand read the gospels, the more convinced he became that he could not mix Jesus together with the gods of Hinduism, most especially since Jesus claimed to be the only path to God, stating: *"I am the Way, the Truth and the*

8

Life. No one comes to the Father except through Me" (John 14:6). In another passage the Bible stated: *"There is one God and one mediator between God and men, the man Christ Jesus who gave Himself a ransom for all."* (1 Tim 2:5-6)

Anand eventually became convinced of the impossibility of coating his Hindu foundation and Communist superstructure with a new layer of Christianity. Through reading the Bible Anand also became aware of his guilt and sinfulness before a pure and holy God. To a Hindu priest and teacher the idea of being a 'sinner' was repulsive. In Anand's own words: *"I never felt myself as a guilty sinner before. According to Hindu philosophy I was completely all right."*

As the days passed by cracks began to appear in Anand's philosophical edifice. Finally, after a long struggle, both intellectually and emotionally, Anand visited his favourite spot by the sea on 23rd January 1954. He had come to an end of his posturing and self-righteousness. Falling on his knees he cast himself on the mercy of God, pleading for forgiveness through the Lord Jesus and surrendering His life to the service of the one true God. The Lord gave him real assurance of the answer to his desperate call:

"I will never forget that experience. I felt such a peace in my heart that everything else was gone. I felt free and utter joy. All the turmoil ceased – the conflict, everything – I was left with just a serene peace, calm and quietness. I experienced my sins being forgiven in a personal way by the only true and holy God through the death of Jesus on the cross. Because He had risen from the dead, He was alive and had given me eternal life. I wanted to tell everyone I met what had happened to me."

Before leaving the beach he removed his priestly Brahmin chord, flinging it as far as he could into the sea. Joyful though he was, the fact is becoming a true Christian was not a soft option

9

for Anand. His change of heart had come after long consideration of the issues involved and there was a price to pay. He took the opportunity to break the news to his relatives at a family reunion at his uncle's house in Bombay. Anand's claim to have met God through Jesus was too much for his father.

"Impossible!" his father retorted, *"The ancient monks spent many years in meditation to gain this experience. Even I have never had it, though I've sought it all my life. How could you, a mere boy, have such an experience?"*

"But it's true father," Anand replied, *"I've been seeking truth for a long time. I even joined the Communists at the university for a time, but they have no morality. Then I began to study the Christian scriptures, and there I found the true holy God – Jesus Christ."*

After an angry outburst, Anand's father lapsed into a stony silence until Anand left Bombay to return home. Tragedy followed shortly afterwards. The next month Anand's parents attended the Kumbh Mela festival at the River Ganges. According to Hindu astrologers, uniquely special powers, only manifested once every 144 years, were to be at work in the sacred river in 1954, enabling the shortening of the devotees' rebirth cycle by 1,000 years. An estimated two to four million people crowded into an 80 acre area by the Ganges hoping for healing, forgiveness and deliverance from the cycle of reincarnation. As the crowd surged forward, Anand's parents and many others were crushed to death. Adding to his overwhelming grief, Anand's relatives blamed the tragic deaths on Anand's conversion to Christ. They saw it as a punishment from the gods and Anand was exiled from the family.

Later he went to a Bible school in Jhansi in the province of Uttar Pradesh where he studied the Bible under Christian lecturers. Now married, Anand preaches the good news of Jesus Christ in various parts of India. He occasionally reflects on the promise his father made at his side while he lay at death's door with smallpox as a child. Could he see him again Anand would assure him:

"Father, I have honoured your promise. I have served God, the only true God, with all my being. He has blessed me far beyond your deepest desires, for I was destined to serve the King of Kings."

CHAPTER 2

Holocaust
(The Testimony of a Jewish Rabbi)

Rabbi Sam Stern
Warsaw, Poland.

I was born at a time when the whole world lay in turmoil - during the 1914-18 World War. I grew up in a strict orthodox Jewish home. Although my parents were poor at that time, they made sacrifices and sent my three brothers and me to a private orthodox school. My father was a devout rabbi who prayed three times a day at the synagogue. His overriding desire in life was to make rabbis of us boys.

By the age of seven I was able to read Hebrew. At nine I was introduced to the five books of Moses, the Bible commentator Rashi and also to the ancient Jewish books of jurisprudence called the Talmud. By the time I reached my eleventh birthday, the Talmud had eclipsed all the other books and became my main textbook from then on. I was under my father's jurisdiction until 13, at which age I was free from his supervision. I was taken to a synagogue where my father thanked God that he was no longer responsible for my sins!

My family lived in a little town in Congress, near Warsaw, Poland. 500 Jewish and 800 Polish families lived there, divided by culture, language and religion. The Jews were not granted the privilege of working for the municipal and federal government,

12

nor in factories and agriculture. We were two peoples living in one territory, under the same Polish sky, eating the same Polish bread and breathing the same Polish air - yet we were as strange to each other as the East is from the West. Growing up I inevitably came into contact with Gentiles. Sometimes they threw stones at me and shouted *"Jew, Jew"*. My mother told me the reason:

"They are Christians and Christians are Jew-haters. But when our Messiah comes, we shall be the head and not the tail. Then we will go back to Palestine and no one will persecute us any more."

"But when will the Messiah come?" I asked.

"We don't know the exact time, but He will come some day. Then our sufferings at the hands of the Christians will come to an end."

The hope of the coming Messiah accompanied me all my life. It gave me power to endure suffering and humiliation from my Gentile neighbours. After my Bar Mitzvah I was sent to a higher rabbinical school. For 9 years I studied the sixty books of the Talmud as I trained to become a Rabbi. By the age of 22 I was considered a 'lamdan' which means a man who is learned in the Talmud.

In September 1939, World War II broke out. I had just received my rabbinical diploma called 'Smicha' that past summer. I had planned to marry and become a religious leader of Israel - to make good use of my acquired knowledge to lead my fellow-Jews in the ways of the Talmudic, rabbinic traditions. An alternative plan was to leave Poland, perhaps to emigrate to a country in Latin America where there was a great need for rabbis. The war destroyed all my plans. My very life was in danger, as was that of all European Jewry. On September 4, the German soldiers came into our town. Life was never to be the same again - it soon became unbearable for Polish Jews. Every Jew was condemned to die. If all the skies were parchment, all men writers, and all trees pens, even then it would not be possible to adequately describe what the Nazis did to the Jews in Poland and the rest of Europe. Within 6 years, 6 million Jews, among them 1 million children, were murdered. One third of the world's Jewish population was annihilated. Yes, here and there a conscientious Polish family rescued a Jew, hiding him and feeding him, but the number of these good people was tragically small.

Finally, in May 1945, the War was over. I was in a Concentration Camp but I had survived. I had high hopes of seeing my relatives again. I put advertisements in newspapers. I went to different institutions. To my great sorrow I learned that all my loved ones had perished. I came to realize the bitter fact that I was alone in the world without a friend - belonging to no one and no one belonging to me. I couldn't believe it; I would never see my parents, my sister, my brothers or my uncles and aunts again. I started to look for a friend in this strange new world, but not surprisingly none could satisfy my longing for a true mother's heart or a father's love. I was disappointed and desperate. I lifted my eyes up to heaven and asked the question - why? Why was one third of the nation of God put to death by the Nazis? Where was God when little innocent Jewish children cried for help and the Nazi murderers raised their brutal hands to kill them? Why was God silent in these terrible times for His chosen people?

Since I had no one in Poland, I decided to go to America. I thought that perhaps in a new land I would forget the dreadful past and start a new life. In order to go to America I had to go first to Germany. In April 1946 I came to a Jewish D.P. Camp near the Austrian border of Germany. I registered there as a rabbi and started to work as such in the D.P. Camp. I also edited the

D.P. Newspaper. Finally, in 1952 I came to Rhode Island, U.S.A., where I worked as an assistant rabbi. Although I worked in the capacity of a Talmudic teacher in the synagogue, there was a great conflict in my heart. The question as to why God had allowed 6 million Jews to die loomed large in my mind - it would not go away.

I taught things I was no longer sure were true. *"If we Jews want to exist and to overcome our enemies we have to keep the Sabbath-day holy,"* I used to say. But in my heart I knew that most of the Hitler-victims had kept the Sabbath-day holy, yet it had not protected them from being killed. I did not have any proof or assurance any more. I lost my belief in the Talmudic legends, laws, and arguments pro and con. I was looking for the truth, but could not find it.

Each holiday we went to the synagogue and prayed to God, confessing our sins, and asking for forgiveness. We said, *"Because of our sins we were driven from our land."* Confession of sins was a very important part of our prayers. The Jewish prayer-book cites different kinds of sins which a Jew must confess in his daily prayers. The most solemn day of prayer is Yom Kippur, one evening of which every Jew over 13 years of age must recite 45 confessions called 'Al Chets'. After the confession, the 'Slach Lanu' (forgive us) is chanted by the congregation.

When I prayed these prayers I felt unhappy and dissatisfied because I knew that according to the Bible, confession alone does not forgive sin. I knew that in order for sin to be forgiven, a sacrifice called 'korban' must be offered. Leviticus deals with the korban many times (see Lev 5:17-19). I was not sure that the Yom Kippur prayers had any significance in the sight of God, because I knew that right after the confessions and prayers we went back to the same old pattern of a life of sin. It seemed to me that as we

15

were confessing our sins in the synagogue, we were mocking God. We spoke with our lips about repentance but didn't really mean it.

I felt very unhappy with my spiritual state of mind. I lost faith in mankind and in the rabbinical legends and teachings. I felt miserable knowing that I, as a rabbi, was teaching the people things that I did not believe. I knew that the Talmudic teachings, sayings, scholastic debates, hair-splitting comments about obsolete damages, laws, rules and regulations regarding Sabbath, Holy Days, clothing and washings, were really of very little significance to us. I realized that we needed a really solid spiritual truth by which to live as Jews. But what was the truth? I did not know. I looked on my people as sheep without a shepherd. I saw that 2,000 years of Talmudic, chasidic, cabbalistic and worldly teachings could not save one Jew from destruction.

One spring evening I walked somewhere in Rhode Island. I looked aimlessly here and there just breathing the fresh spring air. While I strolled, I noticed some young people standing near a shop handing out leaflets. They caught my attention so I took what they were offering. As I could not read English I decided to go into the store to find out what kind of 'sale' they were having. When I went inside I was surprised to see that there was nothing 'on sale'. To my astonishment I noticed every one sitting with eyes closed and heads bowed. *"What is going on here?"* I thought to myself. I waited a while till everybody had finished. A boy came and talked to me, but I did not understand him. I told him that I spoke only German and Yiddish. Through the use of sign language I made a date to come back the next Wednesday. It was arranged that a German-speaking person would come and explain to me what the organization was.

The next Wednesday the German gentleman was waiting for me. He shook my hand warmly and said to me in German,

"This is a mission to the Jews."

"What is a mission?" I asked.

"The Lord sent us to the Jews to let them know that God loves them and wants them to be saved."

"What do you mean saved? How can you speak about love after the cataclysm that came over the European Jew?" I asked.

He smiled and said, *"I know how you feel, but real Christians, followers of Christ, love the Jews, and all those who harm them are not true Christians."*

I retorted, *"Weren't all those who carried crosses and had pictures of saints in their homes - yet organised pogroms against the Jews of Europe - weren't they Christians? Weren't the churches in Poland and Ukraine the main source of anti-Semitism? Didn't the priests incite their people against the Jews?"*

He looked at me and said, *"The Lord teaches us to love our enemies, to show love to those who hate us. All those who do not obey the teachings of the Lord are not His followers."*

Then he gave me a Yiddish New Testament and said, *"Read it and you will find the true teaching of Christ."*

In the next few nights I had much to read. Every line, each page, was a revelation to me. Beginning with the Book of Matthew, I was surprised to read that Jesus is of the lineage of Abraham and David. I also noticed that on nearly every page it says *"As it is written"*, meaning 'written in the Jewish Bible'. For example, in the first chapter I read that the Messiah will be born of a virgin as it is written in Isaiah, *"Behold a virgin shall be with child and shall bring forth a son and you shall call his name Immanuel"* (Isaiah 7:14).

In the 2nd chapter of Matthew I read that the Messiah was to be born in Bethlehem, as it is written: *"And you Bethlehem in the land of Judah are not the least among the princes of Judah, for out of you shall come forth a governor that shall rule my people Israel"* (Micah 5:2). Also I saw that He would visit and return out of Egypt, for it is written: *"Out of Egypt have I called my son"* (Hosea 11:1). It seemed there were constant references to the Old Testament throughout the gospel according to Matthew. It became clear to me that this book called the New Testament is actually the fulfilment of the Old Testament. Right there and then I became a Bible-believing Jew. I thanked God for leading me to that little Mission and decided to dedicate my life to the Messiah.

It was a few weeks before Passover. The missionary in Rhode Island gave me the address of a Jewish believer in Jesus who lived in New York. I had never met such a person before! As soon as I contacted him, he invited me to his home. He greeted me with, *"Shalom Aleichem"*. We read together from the New Testament in Yiddish. After a while he told me he had written a poem called 'The Sufferer' and started to read it. Then he asked me, *"Who is the subject of this poem? Who suffered for our sins? By whose stripes are we healed?"*

I answered, *"It probably refers to Jesus Christ."*

Then he said, *"I just copied out and read to you the 53rd chapter of Isaiah. He was the one who wrote about the Messiah."*

Imagine my surprise and shock. What he had pretended was a poem was actually a chapter from the Jewish Bible. I did not know about Isaiah 53. That day I showed the same 'poem' to a friend in New York. He did not know it was a chapter from Isaiah either. The only conclusion I could reach was that the main reason so many Rabbis and other Jews don't know the Messiah, the Saviour of the Old and New Testament, is that they don't know the Bible.

The same evening I went back to the New York missionary and told him that I believe in the Bible and in the Lord Jesus. We knelt together and prayed for the forgiveness of sin and for salvation. As a repentant sinner I accepted the Lord Jesus as my personal Saviour. What a change came over me - I was so happy! I felt a peace, joy and happiness that I had never known before. I was a new person. When I came home I took the Bible and read the 53rd chapter of Isaiah over and over again. As I read I wondered why I had not heard of Isaiah 53 before. Why didn't the Rabbis tell me about this chapter? It was obvious to me that we Jews could not be considered Bible-believers if we deny Isaiah 53. As I read more, it became clear to me that Isaiah's prophecy in chapter 53 expresses God's glorious plan of forgiveness, reconciliation with God and salvation clearer than perhaps any other passage of scripture.

I went to Los Angeles and started my American education. After finishing 8 grades I graduated from high school. Later I went to Los Angeles City College, and finally to Biola College, where I received a B.A. degree. I was baptized and eventually became a preacher of the Gospel. I had come a long way. With the Lord Jesus as my Messiah it felt like the difference between darkness and light. Ever since that day it has been my one desire that others of my fellow-Jews should also come to know the one spoken of in Isaiah 53.

CHAPTER 3

The Persecuted Professor
(The Testimony of an Imam)

Dr. M. A. Gabriel*
Former Professor of Islamic history
at Al-Azhar University, Cairo, Egypt

The Al-Azhar University in Cairo, Egypt, from which I graduated, is the oldest and most prestigious Islamic University in the world. It serves as the spiritual authority for Islam worldwide. I taught there during the week and performed the duties of an Imam at the weekend at a Mosque in the city of Giza, Egypt (where the pyramids are located). Among other responsibilities, I used to preach each Friday from noon to 1pm.

One particular Friday my topic concerned 'Jihad'. I told my large audience: *"Jihad means defending Islam against the attacks of the enemies. Islam is a religion of peace and will only fight against one who fights it. These infidels, heathens, Christians and Allah's grievers, the Jews, out of envy of peaceful Islam and its prophet, spread the myth that Islam is promulgated by the sword. These accusers of Islam, do not acknowledge Allah's words."* I quoted from the Qur'an: *"And do not kill anyone whom Allah has forbidden, except for a just cause"* (Surah 17:33). My sermon was in line with the philosophy of the Egyptian government. Al-Azhar University focused on politically correct Islam and overlooked areas of Islamic teaching that conflicted with its chosen interpretation. Outwardly I

20

preached what they taught me, but inside, confusion reigned. I knew that to keep my position at Al-Azhar, I needed to keep my thoughts to myself, only too aware of what happened to people who differed from Al-Azhar's agenda. A dismissal would have rendered me 'unfit' to teach at *any* University in the nation. Yet I knew that my sermons on Jihad at the Mosque and at Al-Azhar conflicted with the Qur'an, all of which I had memorized by the age of twelve. How could I preach about an Islam of love and forgiveness, while Muslim fundamentalists – the ones claiming to be practising true Islam – were regularly bombing churches and killing Christians?

Although not personally involved in anything radical, one of my Muslim friends, a chemistry student, belonged to an Islamic group active in slaughtering Christians. One day I asked him, "*Why are you killing our neighbours and countrymen with whom we grew up.*" He was angry and astonished at my challenge. "*Out of all Muslims* you *should know. The Christians do not accept the call of Islam and they are not willing to pay us the jizyah* [tax] *to have the right to practise their beliefs. Therefore, the only option they have is the sword of Islamic law.*"

My conversations with him drove me to pore over the Qur'an and the books of Islamic law, hoping to find something to contradict what he said. I soon realized I had two basic options. I could continue to embrace a 'Christianized' form of Islam – an Islam of peace, love and compassion – thereby keeping my job and status; or I could become a member of the Islamic movement and embrace the Islam of the Qur'an, based on the teachings of Muhammad. I had tried to rationalize the kind of Islam to which I held. After all, there are verses in the Qur'an about love, peace and compassion. Conveniently ignoring the parts about Jihad, I sought out interpretations of the Qur'an that did not advocate the killing of non-Muslims, yet I kept finding support of the practice. Islamic scholars agreed that Muslims should enforce Jihad on infidels and renegades. These contradictions in the Qur'an presented a real

21

stumbling block to my faith.

I spent four years earning my Bachelor's degree, graduating second out of a class of 6,000. Then another four years for my Master's and three more for my Doctorate – all in Islamic studies. That's why I knew the contradictions in the Qur'an so well. In one place alcohol was forbidden; in another it was allowed (compare Surah 5:90–91 with Surah 47:15). In one place it says Christians are good people who love and worship one God (Surah 2:62, 3:113–114), but you find other verses that say Christians must convert, pay tax or be killed by the sword (Surah 9:29-30). In one place man is said to have been made from water (Surah 21:30); in another he comes from a blood clot (Surah 96:1-2); in yet another from dust (Surah 3:58). Certainly the scholars had theological 'solutions' to these problems, but I wondered how Allah, almighty and all powerful, could either contradict himself or at least change his mind so much. Even the prophet of Islam, Muhammad, practised his faith in ways that contradicted the Qur'an. The Qur'an said that Muhammad was sent to show the mercy of God to the world, but he became a military dictator, attacking, killing and taking plunder to finance his empire. Then, again, Islam is full of discrimination – against women, against non-Muslims, against Christians and most especially against Jews. Hatred is built in to the religion. The history of Islam, which was my special area of study, could only be described as a river of blood.

Inevitably I reached the point where I questioned Islam and the Qur'an with my students at the University. Some of them, members of terrorist movements, were enraged: "*You can't accuse Islam. What has happened to you? You must agree with Islam.*" The university heard about it so I was called in for a meeting in December 1991. I told them what was in my heart: "*I can no longer say that the Qur'an comes directly from heaven or from Allah. It cannot be the revelation of the true God.*" To them my words were nothing short of blasphemy. They spat in my face. One man cursed me; "*You blasphemer. You bastard.*" The University fired me and called the Egyptian secret police.

My whole family lived together in a three-storey house – my parents, my four married brothers with their families, my unmarried brother and myself. Only my married sister lived elsewhere. The house was divided into several comfortable apartments, with my brother and I sharing the ground floor with our parents. At three o'clock in the morning the next day my father heard knocking at the door of our house. When he opened the door, fifteen to twenty men rushed in carrying assault weapons. They were not wearing uniforms. They ran all through the house, waking people up looking for me. I had nowhere to hide. My family was terrified. They wept as I was dragged away. Everybody in the area heard the commotion.

Later that morning my parents frantically tried to figure out what had happened to me. They went to the Police Station and demanded, "*Where is our son?* " But nobody knew anything about me. The Egyptian secret Police saw to that. They put me in a cell with two radical Muslims accused of committing terrorist acts. One, a Palestinian, the other, an Egyptian. For three days I was denied food and water. The Egyptian constantly asked me, "*Why are you here?* " I refused to answer, afraid he would kill me if he knew that I harboured questions about Islam. On the third day, I told him I taught at Al-Azhar University and held the position of an Imam in Giza. Immediately he gave me a plastic bottle of water and some falafel and pita that were brought to him by his own visitors, despite the Police warning him not to give me anything. On the fourth day, the interrogation began, the goal of which seemed to be to make me confess my rebellion against Islam.

My interrogator sat behind a large desk. Behind me were two or three police officers. He felt sure that my conversion to

Christianity involved someone else. *"What pastor did you talk to?"* he demanded. *"What church have you been visiting? Why have you betrayed Islam?"* The questions seemed endless. On one question I hesitated too long before answering. My inter-rogator nodded to the men behind me. They grabbed my hand and held it down on the desk. My interrogator took a lit cigarette, reached over and extinguished it into the top of my hand. The scar is there to this day. So is the scar on my lip, where I received the same treatment. The pressure increased with time. One officer pressed a red-hot poker into the flesh of my left arm. They wanted me to confess that I had been converted, but I said, *"I didn't betray Islam. I just said what I believe. I am an academic person. I am a thinker. I have a right to discuss any subject of Islam. This is part of my job and part of any academic life. I could not even dream of converting from Islam – it is my blood, my culture, my language, my family, my life. But if you accuse me of converting from Islam for what I say to you, then take me out of Islam. I don't mind being out of Islam."*

My answer didn't please them. I was taken to a room containing a steel bed. They tied my feet to the foot of the bed and then put heavy stockings on them. An officer with a four foot long whip began lashing my feet. I was beaten unconscious. When I woke up the officer stopped and untied me. *"Stand up,"* he demanded. I could not at first, but he beat my back until I complied with his request. He pointed down a long passageway. *"Run,"* he bellowed. Again, when I could not do it, he whipped my back until I ran down the passageway. When I reached the end, there was another officer waiting for me. He whipped me until I ran back. They made me run back and forth repeatedly. Then I was put in a tank full of ice-cold water. I have low blood sugar, so it wasn't very long before I passed out again. When I awoke I was lying on the steel bed, still in my wet clothes.

Further tortures followed. The officers took me to the door of a small room and said, *"There is someone in there who loves you very much and wants to meet you."* I was hoping it might be a family member or a friend. They opened the door. Inside I saw nothing but a large dog. The door shut behind me. I cried out from my heart to my Creator, *"You are my father, my God. Please look after me. Can you leave me in these evil hands? I don't know what these people are trying to do to me, but I know you will be with me and one day I will see you and meet you."* I walked to the middle of the room and slowly sat down cross-legged on the floor. The dog came and sat down in front of me. Then it started circling me, as if preparing to eat me. To my relief it simply sat down and stayed by my side. I was so exhausted I fell asleep. When I woke up, the dog was in the corner of the room. When the officers finally opened the door they saw me praying, with the dog sitting next to me. I heard one say, *"I can't believe this man is a human being. This man is a devil – he's Satan."*

"I don't believe that," the other replied, *"There is an unseen power standing behind this man and protecting him."*

The first officer concluded; *"What power? This man is an infidel. It's got to be Satan because this man is against Allah."*

In my absence, my Egyptian cellmate asked the police, *"Why are you persecuting this man?"* They told him, *"Because he is denying Islam."* He was furious. When I rejoined him in the cell, he was ready to kill me. But I had only been in there twenty minutes when a police officer came with transfer papers for him and he was taken away. *"What is going on here?"* I thought to myself, *"What power is protecting me?"* At that time, I did not know the answer. Shortly thereafter my own transfer papers came through. My destiny? A permanent prison in southern Cairo. All of this for merely 'questioning' Islam. My faith was really shaken.

My first week in Cairo was relatively relaxed. Thankfully my prison guard did not agree with radical Islam. Throughout this whole time my family persisted in trying to find out my whereabouts. They had no success until my mother's brother, who was a high-ranking member of the Egyptian Parliament, returned to the country from travelling overseas. My mother called him, sobbing, *"For two weeks we have not known where our son is. He is gone."* My uncle had the necessary connections. Fifteen days after I was kidnapped, he came to the prison personally with release papers and took me home.

Later, the police gave a report to my father: *"We have received a fax from Al-Azhar University accusing your son of leaving Islam, but after an interrogation of fifteen days, we found no evidence to support it."* My father was relieved to hear this. I was the only one in the family who had studied Islam at the University, and he was very proud of me. That I would ever leave Islam was, to my father, unimaginable. He attributed the whole incident to jealousy. *"We don't need them,"* he said, and then asked me to start work immediately as a sales director in his successful clothing manufacturing business.

For the following year I lived in a vacuum. I had no faith, no God to pray to, to call on, to live for. I believed in the existence of a God who was merciful and righteous but I had no idea who He was. Was He the God of the Muslims, the Christians or the Jews? Or was He some animal – like the cow of the Hindus? I had no idea how to find Him. If a Muslim concludes that Islam is not the truth, where can he turn? Faith is in the fabric of the life of a Middle Eastern person. He cannot imagine life without God. The events of that year took their toll. I was constantly tired and suffered continually from headaches. I began visiting a nearby pharmacy one or two times a week to buy a packet of tablets. After a while, the pharmacist asked me, *"What is going on in your life?"*

"Nothing is going on," I answered. *"I have no complaint except for one thing: I am living without God. I don't know who God is, who created me and the universe."*

26

Startled, she said, *"But you were a professor at the most respected Islamic University in Egypt. Your family is very respected in the community."*

"That is true," I replied. *"But I have discovered falsehoods in their teachings. I no longer believe my home and family are built on a foundation of truth. I had always clothed myself in the lies of Islam. Now I feel naked. How can I fill the emptiness in my heart? Please help me."*

"OK." she said. *"Today I will give you these tablets, and I will give you this book – the Bible. But please promise me not to take any tablets before you read something from this book."*

I took the book home and opened it at random. My eyes fell on Matthew 5:38: *"You have heard that it was said, An eye for an eye, and a tooth for a tooth, but I tell you not to resist an evil person. But whoever slaps you on your right cheek, turn the other to Him also."* I began to tremble. I had studied the Qur'an my whole life – not once had I found anything like this. I had come face to face with the Lord Jesus Christ.

As I continued to read I lost all track of time. It felt as if I was sitting on a cloud above a hill, while in front of me was the greatest teacher in the Universe revealing all the secrets of heaven to me. Compared to what I had learned from my years of studying the Qur'an, there was no doubt in my mind that here, in the Bible, I was finally encountering the true God. I read into the early hours of the next day and by dawn I had repented and received Jesus Christ as my Lord and Saviour, believing that He died for my sins and rose again from the dead. The only people I told were the Pharmacist and his wife. In Egypt, if anyone leaves Islam, it is automatically assumed that he has become a Christian and therefore must be killed.

Somehow the news leaked out. The fundamentalists sent two men to ambush and kill me. While returning home on foot from a social visit to a friend's house about a twenty minute walk away in

Giza, I was on Tersae Street, near my home, when I saw two men standing in front of a grocery shop. Dressed traditionally in white robes, long beards and head coverings, I thought they must be customers. However, as I reached the shop they stopped me and pulled out knives with which to stab me. I put up my hands to protect myself. Again and again the blades struck me, cutting my wrists. The other people in the street gathered to watch but no one helped me. The first attacker was trying to stab my heart. He missed and penetrated my shoulder instead. When he pulled the knife out I fell to the ground in a little ball, trying to protect myself. The other attacker tried to stab me in the stomach, but the blade turned, and he stabbed me in the shin instead. I passed out. Apparently two police officers arrived on motorcycles and my attackers ran away. I was taken to the hospital and treated. Again, my father rejected any thought that I was abandoning Islam. He just could not think in those terms.

I continued to work for my father but never spoke of my new faith. In fact, he sent me to South Africa in 1994 to explore business opportunities for him. While there, I spent three days with a Christian family from India. When we parted, they gave me a small cross on a necklace to wear. This small cross marked the turning point in my life. After a little more than a week back home, my father noticed it. *"Why do you wear this chain?"* he demanded.

"Father, this is not a chain," I explained. *"This is a cross. It represents Jesus, who died on a cross for me, for you and for everybody in the whole world. I have received Jesus as my God and Saviour, and I pray for you and for the rest of my family to also repent and receive Jesus Christ as your Lord and Saviour."*

My father collapsed in the street. Some of my brothers rushed out and brought him into the house. My mother started crying in fear. I stayed with them as they bathed my father's face with water. When he came to, he was so upset he could hardly speak,

28

but he pointed at me. In a voice hoarse with rage he cried out, *"Your brother is a convert. I must kill him today!"* Wherever he went, my father carried a gun under his arm on a leather strap. He pulled out his gun and pointed it at me. I started running down the street and, as I dived around a corner, I heard the bullets. I ran to my sister's house about half a mile away. I asked her to help me get my passport, clothes and other documents from my father's house. She wanted to know what was wrong, and I told her, *"Father wants to kill me."* She asked why. I said, *"I don't know. You must ask Father."*

When I ran away, my father guessed where I was headed because my sister and I were very close. He walked to her house, arriving while we were talking. He banged on the door. He was openly sobbing with tears streaming down his face, *"My daughter, please open the door."* Then he shouted, *"Your brother is a convert! He has left the Islamic faith. I must kill him now!"*

My sister opened the door and tried to calm him down. *"Father, he is not here. Maybe he went to another place. Why don't you go home and later we can talk about this as a family."*

My sister had mercy on me and gathered my things from my parents' house. She and my mother gave me some money. I left on the evening of August 28, 1994. For three months I struggled through Northern Egypt, Libya, Chad and Cameroon. I finally stopped in the Congo where I contracted malaria. I found an Egyptian doctor to examine me. He said that I would be dead by morning and made arrangements to get a coffin from Congo's Egyptian embassy to send me back home. To their shock, I survived the night. I left the hospital after five days.

Ten years have gone by since I was saved from my sins and received peace with God through the Lord Jesus Christ. He called me and gave me a personal relationship with Him – something that

Islam never offered. There is a statement about God in the Bible which is unique. It says *"God so loved the world, that He gave His only begotten Son, that whoever believes in Him, should not perish, but have everlasting life"* (John 3:16). In Islam you must love Allah in order for Allah to love you in return. Surah 3:30 states *"If you love God…God will love you."* In the Bible however, God loves sinners first in order to secure their salvation. *"We* [believers in Jesus] *love Him because He first loved us"* (I John 4:19). *"But God demonstrates His own love toward us, in that while we were still sinners, Christ died for us"* (Rom 5:8). May my life story help you to appreciate and accept this unique love and grace.

* *Dr. Gabriel is not the Professor's birth name. After four years of persecution in South Africa, subsequent to his conversion to Christ, he decided to change his name for security reasons. He chose the name 'Mark' because tradition says that the early disciple of Christ called Mark, who wrote one of the four gospels, was the first person to bring the gospel to Egypt after the resurrection of Jesus.*

CHAPTER 4

From Tradition to Truth

(The Testimony of a Catholic Priest)

Richard Peter Bennett
Texas, USA

Born into a large Irish family my early childhood was fulfilled and happy. My siblings and I loved to play, sing and act, all within a military camp in Dublin. My father was a colonel in the Irish Army until his retirement shortly before I turned ten years of age.

One could say we were a typical Irish Catholic family. My father would sometimes solemnly kneel down to pray at his bedside; mother would talk to Jesus while sewing, washing dishes or even smoking a cigarette. Most evenings we would kneel in the living room to say the Rosary together. Barring serious illness, no one ever missed Sunday Mass. By the time I was about five or six years of age Jesus Christ was a very real person to me, but so also were Mary and the saints. I can readily identify with Catholics from all over the world who turn variously to Jesus, Mary, Joseph and numerous saints in the kaleidoscope of the faith I loved so dearly. The catechism was drilled into me at the Jesuit School of Belvedere where I had gained both my elementary and secondary education. Like every boy who studies under the Jesuits, by the age of ten I could recite from memory five reasons why God exists and why the Pope was head of the only true Church.

Getting souls out of Purgatory was a serious business. I memorized the often quoted words, "It is a holy and a wholesome thought to pray for the dead that they may be loosed from sins," though I did not understand their meaning. As to all Catholics, the Pope was the most important man in the world to me. What he said was law and the Jesuits were his right hand men. I was intrigued by the deep sense of mystery which surrounded the Mass and attempted to attend it daily even though it was in Latin. We had patron saints for most aspects of life and praying to them was encouraged. The only one I prayed to was St. Anthony, the patron of lost objects, since I always seemed to be losing things.

When I was fourteen years old I sensed a call to be a missionary but did not take any action. I enjoyed my teens and did well both academically and athletically. I often had to drive my mother to the hospital for treatments and one day while waiting for her I found some Bible verses quoted in a book in the doctor's surgery: *"And Jesus answered and said, 'Verily I say unto you, there is no man that hath left house, or brethren, or sister, or father, or mother, or wife, or children, or lands, for my sake, and the gospel's, but he shall receive an hundredfold now in this time, houses, and brethren, and sisters, and mothers, and children, and lands, with persecutions; and in the world to come eternal life "* (Mark 10:29-30). That struck me and brought back my earlier impressions of a call to serve God. I made up my mind to be a missionary.

I left my family and friends in 1956 to join the Dominican Order and spent eight years studying what it is to be a monk. I was taught the traditions of the Church, philosophy, the theology of Thomas Aquinas, and some parts of the Bible from a Catholic standpoint. Whatever personal subjective faith I had became

32

institutionalized and ritualized by my experience in the Dominican religious system. Obedience to the law, both Church and Dominican, was put before me as the means of sanctification. I often spoke to Ambrose Duffy, our Master of Students, about how the law could assist me to become holy. In addition to becoming holy I wanted also to be sure of eternal salvation. I memorized some of the teachings of Pope Pius XII in which he said, "...the salvation of many depends on the prayers and sacrifices of the mystical body of Christ offered for this intention." This message of gaining salvation through suffering and prayer was also the basic message of Fatima and Lourdes, and I sought to win my own salvation as well as the salvation of others by such suffering and prayer.

In the Dominican monastery in Tallaght, Dublin, I performed many difficult feats to 'win souls', such as taking a cold shower in the middle of winter and beating my back with a small steel chain. The Master of Students knew what I was doing. His own austere life inspired me to press on with rigour and determination to study, pray, do penance and try to keep the Ten Commandments and the multitude of the Dominicans' rules and traditions.

Finally in 1963, at the age of twenty-five, I was ordained as a Catholic priest and eventually finished my course of studies of Thomas Aquinas at the Angelicum University in Rome. It was in Rome that I first had pause to have second thoughts about my faith. I had difficulty with both the outward pomp and the inner emptiness I saw in the Vatican. Over the years I had formed pictures in my mind of the Holy See and the Holy City. Could this be the same city? In my innocence I was shocked at the hundreds who poured into morning classes at the Angelicum University who seemed quite disinterested in theology. I noticed *Time* and *Newsweek* magazines being read during classes. Those who showed interest seemed only to be looking for degrees and positions within the Catholic Church in their home lands, rather than having a genuine interest in the truth.

One day I went for a walk in the Colosseum, dressed in my religious habit. I wanted to tread the sacred soil where the blood of so many Christian martyrs had been shed. As I entered the arena I tried to picture in my mind those men and women who had known Christ so well that they had joyfully given their bodies to be burned at the stake or to be devoured by beasts. The joy of this experience was marred during the bus ride back to the University. I was insulted by jeering Catholic youths shouting at me "Scum and garbage." I felt I was a target for their jibes not because I stood for Christ as the early Christians had, but because they saw me as a priest of the Church. What I had been taught about the 'glories of Rome' now seemed very hollow and a sham. Shortly after this experience I prayed for two hours one night in front of the main altar in the church of San Clemente. Remembering before the Lord my earlier youthful call to be a missionary and the hundredfold promise of Mark 10:29-30, I decided to abandon my ambition of gaining a theological degree in the study of the theology of Thomas Aquinas. After long prayer I felt at peace about this major decision.

The priest whose responsibility it was to direct my thesis refused to accept my decision. To make the degree easier, he offered to give me a copy of a thesis written several years earlier. He said I could use it as my own if only I would do the oral defence of dissertation. This really turned my stomach. I was offended by the sheer hypocrisy this offer represented. I stuck by my decision and left the university at the ordinary academic level, without my degree. On returning to Ireland, I received official word that I had been assigned to do a three year course at Cork University. I continued to pray earnestly about my missionary call and, to my surprise, I received orders in late August 1964 to go to Trinidad, West Indies.

On October 1, 1964, I arrived in Trinidad, and for seven years successfully performed all my priestly duties. By 1972 I had become quite involved in the Catholic Charismatic Movement in the West Indies. Then on March 16th of that year at a prayer meeting, I thanked the Lord that I was such a good priest and requested that if it were His will that He humble me that I might serve Him even better. Later that same evening I had a freak accident, splitting the back of my head and hurting my spine in numerous places. Coming close to death shook me out of my self-satisfied state. Rote, or set prayer, proved useless as I cried out to God in my pain.

During the weeks after my accident I found some comfort in direct personal prayer. I stopped saying the Breviary (the Catholic Church's official prayer for clergy) and the Rosary and slowly began to pray using parts of the Bible itself. I did not know my way through the Bible. The little I had learned about it over the years had led me to distrust it. My training in philosophy and in the theology of Thomas Aquinas left me helpless in my hour of need. Coming to the Bible now to find the Lord was like going into a huge dark wood without a map.

When assigned to the parish of Pointe-a-Pierre later that year, I found that I was to work for more than two years side-by-side with a Dominican priest who had been like a brother to me over the years. We read, studied, prayed and put into practice what we had been taught by the Church. We built up Catholic communities in Gasparillo, Claxton Bay and in Marabella, just to mention the main villages. We were hugely successful in our labours. Many people attended Mass. The Catechism was taught in many schools, including government schools. I continued my personal search into the Bible, but it hardly affected the work we were doing. How little I really knew about the Lord and His Word! It was at this time that Philippians 3:10 became the cry of my heart, *"That I may know Him, and the power of His resurrection…"*

We introduced the growing Catholic Charismatic movement into most of our villages. News of our success brought some Canadian Christians to Trinidad to help us. From their messages I learned much, especially about prayers for healing. Though the whole emphasis of their teaching was experience-orientated, it had the effect of pointing me to the Bible as an authority source. I started to compare one scripture with another and even to quote chapter and verse! One of the texts the Canadians used to urge us to pray for healing was Isaiah 53:5, *"…and with his stripes we are healed."* Yet as I studied Isaiah 53, I discovered that it focuses on sin rather than on healing. It says, *"All like sheep have gone astray; we have turned every one to his own way; and the LORD hath laid on him the iniquity of us all"* (Isaiah 53:6).

One of my besetting sins was pride. I was easily annoyed with people, sometimes becoming angry and impatient with them. Although I asked forgiveness for my sins, I still did not realize that I was a sinner by nature, a nature I had inherited from our first parents, Adam and Eve. The Bible says, *"As it is written, There is none righteous, no, not one"*, and *"All have sinned, and come short of the glory of God"* (Romans 3:23). The Catholic Church, however, had taught me that the depravity of man, which is called 'original sin', had been washed away by my infant baptism. I still held this belief in my head, but in my heart I knew that my depraved nature had not yet been conquered by Christ. *'That I may know Him, and the power of His resurrection…'* (Philippians 3:10) continued to be the cry of my heart; I knew that it could be only through His power that I could live the Christian life. I posted this text on the dashboard of my car and in other places. It became the plea that motivated me, and the Lord who is Faithful began to answer.

First, I discovered that God's Word in the Bible is absolute and without error. I had been taught that the Word is relative and that its truthfulness in many areas was to be questioned. Now I began to understand that the Bible could in fact be trusted. With the aid of Strong's Concordance, I began to study the Bible to see what it says about itself. I discovered that the Bible teaches clearly that it is from God and is absolute in what it says. It is true in its history, in the promises God has made, in its prophecies, in the moral commands it gives, and in how to live the Christian life. *'All scripture is given by inspiration of God, and is profitable for doctrine, for reproof, for correction, for instruction in righteousness: That the man of God may be perfect, thoroughly furnished unto all good works.'* (II Timothy 3:16-17)

This discovery was made while visiting in Vancouver, B.C., and in Seattle. When I was asked to talk to the prayer group in St. Stephen's Catholic Church, I took as my subject the absolute authority of God's Word. It was the first time that I had talked about such a truth. After the teaching, I prayed for a lady there who since childhood had an eye problem. The Lord healed her. I took this to mean that the Lord was confirming the truth of what I had come to understand about the absolute nature of His Word. I became close friends with the lady who had been healed, and her husband. Her healing has continued to this present day. This new discovery regarding the nature of the Word of God I now see as pivotal in my life. Let me say, however, that I do not take miracles as an authority source, for there is one source of authority, that is, God's Word. Rather I tell about the miracle because this is why it happened. God is sovereign.

While I was still parish priest of Point-a-Pierre, Ambrose Duffy, the man who had so strictly taught me while he was Student Master, was asked to assist me. The tide had turned. After some initial difficulties, we became close friends. I shared with him what I was discovering. He listened and commented with great interest and wanted to find out what was motivating me. I saw in him a channel to my Dominican brothers and even to those in the Archbishop's house. When he died suddenly of a heart attack, I was stricken with grief. In my mind, I had seen Ambrose as the one who could make sense out of the Church-Bible dilemma with which I so struggled. I had hoped that he would have been able to explain to me and then to my Dominican brothers the truths with which I wrestled. I preached at his funeral and my despair was very deep.

I continued to pray Philippians 3:10, *'That I may know Him, and the power of His resurrection...'* But to learn more about Him, I had first to learn about myself as a sinner. I saw from the Bible (I Timothy 2:5) that the role I was playing as a priestly mediator – exactly what the Catholic Church teaches, but exactly opposite to what the Bible teaches – was wrong. I really enjoyed being looked up to by the people, and, in a certain sense, being idolized by them. I rationalized my sin by saying that after all if this is what the biggest Church in the world teaches, who am I to question it? Still, I struggled with the conflict inside myself. I began to see the worship of Mary, the saints, and the priests for the sin that it is. But while I was willing to renounce Mary and the saints as mediators, I could not renounce the priesthood, for in that I had my whole life invested.

Mary, the saints, and the priesthood was just a small part of the huge struggle with which I was working. Who was Lord of my life, Jesus Christ in His Word, or the Catholic Church? This ultimate question raged inside me especially during my last six years as parish priest of Sangre Grande (1979-1985). That the Catholic Church was supreme in all matters of faith and morals had been dyed into my brain since I was a child. It looked impossible to ever change. Rome was not only supreme, but always called 'Holy Mother'. How could I ever go against 'Holy Mother,' all the more so since I had an official part in dispensing her sacraments and keeping people faithful to her?

In 1981, I actually rededicated myself to serving the Church while attending a parish renewal seminar in New Orleans. Yet when I returned to Trinidad and again became involved in real life problems I began to return to the authority of God's Word. Finally the tension became like a war inside me. Sometimes I looked to the Catholic Church as being absolute, sometimes the authority of the Bible as being final. My stomach suffered much during those years; my emotions were being torn. I ought to have known the simple truth that one cannot serve two masters. My working position was to place the absolute authority of the Word of God under the supreme authority of the Catholic Church.

This contradiction was symbolized in what I did with the four statues in the Sangre Grande church. I removed and broke up the statues of St. Francis and St. Martin because the second commandment declares in Exodus 20:4, *'Thou shalt not make unto thee any graven image...'* But when some of the people objected to my removal of the statues of the Sacred Heart and of Mary, I left them standing, because the higher authority, i.e., the Catholic Church, said in this law Canon 1188: 'The practice of displaying sacred images in the churches for the veneration of the faithful is to remain in force.' I did not see that what I was trying to do was to make God's Word subject to man's word.

While I had learned earlier that God's Word is absolute, I still went through this agony of trying to maintain the Catholic

39

Church as holding more authority than God's Word, even in issues where the Church of Rome was saying the exact opposite to what is in the Bible. How could this be? First of all, it was my own fault. If I had accepted only the authority of the Bible as supreme, I would have been convicted by God's Word to give up my priestly role as mediator, but that was too precious to me. Second, no one ever questioned what I did as a priest. Christians from overseas came to Mass, saw our sacred oils, holy water, medals, statues, vestments, rituals, and never said a word! The marvellous style, symbolism, music, and artistic taste of the Catholic Church were all very captivating. Incense not only smells pungent, but to the mind it spells mystery.

One day, a woman challenged me (the only Christian ever to challenge me in all my 22 years as a priest), 'You Catholics have a form of godliness, but you deny its power.' Those words bothered me for some time, because the lights, banners, folk music, guitars, and drums were dear to me. Probably no priest on the whole island of Trinidad had as colourful robes, banners, and vestments as I had. Clearly I did not apply what was before my eyes.

In October 1985, God's grace was greater than the lie that I was trying to live. I went to Barbados to pray over the compromise that I was forcing myself to live. I felt truly trapped. The Word of God is absolute indeed - that alone ought I to obey; yet to the very same God I had vowed obedience to the supreme authority of the Catholic Church. In Barbados I read a book that commented on the well know text of Matthew 16:18 in which the Lord says '...I will build my church...' In the Lord's own language, the word church is 'eda' meaning 'fellowship.' I had always taken the meaning of 'church' to be 'supreme teaching authority in all matters of faith and morals.' Now to see and to understand the meaning of church as 'fellowship' left me free to let go of the

40

Catholic Church as supreme authority, and to depend on Jesus Christ as Lord. It began to dawn on me that in Biblical terms the Bishops I knew in the Catholic Church were not Biblical believers. They were for the most part pious men taken up with devotion to Mary and the Rosary, and loyal to Rome, but not one had any idea of the finished work of salvation, that Christ's work is done, that salvation is personal and complete. They all preached penance for sin, human suffering, religious deeds, 'the way of man' rather than the Gospel of grace. But by God's grace I saw that it was not the Catholic Church nor by any kind of works that one is saved, *'For by grace are ye saved through faith; and that not of yourselves: it is the gift of God: Not of works, lest any man should boast'* (Ephesians 2:8-9).

I suffered for fourteen years, no one ever having the courage to speak the truth to me. I share these truths with you now so that you can know God's way of salvation. I pray that the Father will give you grace that you may accept that Christ died in your place on the cross, and know that His atonement is sufficient to make you a new creature in Him: *"For God so loved the world, that He gave His only-begotten Son, that whosoever believeth in Him should not perish, but have everlasting life."* (John 3:16)

CHAPTER 5

A Tibetan's Story
(The Testimony of a Buddhist Monk)

Hyima Chothar
Tibet

Nyima Chothar served as a Tibetan Buddhist monk for thirty two years from 1923 to 1955. He relates his early memories of his childhood in Tibet:

"In the fire-serpent year of the 15th rabchung (1917) in the little village of Churn in Namling county, I was born into a farming family. Until I was six years old, I lived with my parents and sisters at home. When I was small I used to play at being a monk: beating the drums, blowing the white conch-shell, setting up the special offerings called tormas, and imitating the sacred dances. My parents encouraged me by giving me red and yellow clothing just like the monks wear. Before I was seven, my parents went to their master to ask permission for me to enter the monastery. In former times in Tibet there were many landholders and lords, and the common people, without any power of their own, had to live under their authority. One could not just decide to become a monk on one's own – one had to ask permission. Hence my parents had to seek their lord's permission for me to become a monk."

Nyima's uncle enrolled him in the monastery at Ganden Chokhor where he looked after him.

"From the time I was eight until I was eleven I studied the Tibetan language, plus a whole course of study known as Chojo Rabsel, on which all monks have to pass an examination. Though I didn't have to, I also took an examination on the Gyan Juk (a book of Buddhist philosophy) and ten chapters of another book called Cho Juk (known in English as Santideva's 'Guide to the Boddhisattva's Way of Life'). Of sixty boys who took the exam, I had the good fortune to receive first place prize, an 'a-she khatag' or Tibetan ceremonial scarf."

Nyima later asked his parents if he could have permission to go to Lhasa. "When I reached Lhasa I stayed in Sera Monastery's Je College, where about thirty monks from Ganden Chokhor were studying Buddhist philosophy. There for two years I diligently studied the scriptural commentaries called Namdel, and the Buddhist Scriptures known as Prajnaparamita."

As he grew in his understanding and knowledge of Buddhism, he began to serve his people. "I went out into Lhasa and the nearby villages to recite Buddhist texts. Sometimes, when someone had died, I went to recite the text known as the Bardo Thodol. Tibetans believe that at death a person's spirit wanders in an intermediate state called the Bardo, before being reborn (reincarnation). During this time, the person's spirit is terrified by visions of wrathful gods. By hearing this scripture, it is believed that the person can be delivered from fear; hence the name Bardo Thodol (which means 'deliverance through hearing in the Bardo'). By conducting such ceremonies, a monk receives gifts of food and money, so much so that he doesn't need to do any other kind of work. Often young monks don't think about the needs of the sick and the dying, but only about the money they receive for services rendered. Other privileges were available to me as a monk. On many occasions I had to go to Lhasa's Nechung Monastery for ceremonies involving the worship of the goddess Dolma. At

Nechung lived the State Oracle, a man whom the Tibetans believe can see into the future."

The Dalai Lama is a lineage of religious officials of the Gelug sect of Tibetan Buddhism. The Dalai Lama is believed by his devotees to be the rebirth of a long line of tulkus who descend from the bodhisattva Avalokite☐vara. The current Dalai Lama, 'His Holiness', is thought of as the latest reincarnation of a series of spiritual leaders who have chosen to be reborn in order to enlighten others. Between the 17th century and 1959, the Dalai Lamas were the directors of the Tibetan Government, administering a large portion of the area from the capital Lhasa. Since 1959, the Dalai Lama has been the president of the Tibetan government-in-exile. For a year Nyima had the privilege of being a servant to the Dalai Lama's personal bodyguard at the Potala. For other people it was difficult to see or meet the Dalai Lama, but Hyima saw him every day. At that time he was about thirteen or fourteen years old. It was then that he took to the life of a pilgrim monk, travelling through Tibet and visiting other monasteries. He also travelled through Bhutan and parts of India. In 1950, he had an experience which deeply unsettled him. He writes:

"On the fourth day of the sixth Tibetan month is the festival commemorating the preaching of the Buddha's first sermon. Early in the morning the monks and nuns and former monks of that area come together to worship the goddess Dolma. In the evening all of us drank Tibetan beer and hard liquor until we were out of our minds. That night four of us broke our monastic vows with Bhutanese women. Feeling very sad, and knowing that I'd shamed my parents, I didn't want to stay there any more. I felt deep regret, but there was no way to repent and take it back. To have thought ahead would have been wise; to feel sorry about it later was stupid."

Hyima became pretty disillusioned not only at his own behaviour but at the generally low standard of his fellow monks' morals, with their frequent gambling, drunkenness and immorality. In 1951, while on the way back to Tibet from Bhutan, he fell sick with malaria and found help in a Christian hospital run by the Finnish Mission at Baxaduars. The Christians there cared for him. He noted that they were not only very kind but that their morals were of a higher standard than he was used to among the monks. As he recovered, Miss Hellin Hukka, a Finnish lady, exchanged some of his Buddhist books for a Bible. Its contents were totally new to him.

"In the Bible they'd given me, I read about the God who made the sky, the earth, the ocean, the trees and all that is in the world. There it was written that God created the earth's birds and animals and all the ocean's creatures. The Bible said that God made the first man and woman, and that by disobeying God's command these two people became sinners. Their sin was passed on to all their offspring, making us all sinners. But according to our Buddhist religion, the world arose by itself. A monkey, the emanation of the god Chenresi, was the father of all men, and a rock-demoness, the emanation of the goddess Dolma, was the mother of all. That was the way mankind began. I had to think about which version of events was true. Even if that monkey could be the father of mankind, how could the rock-demoness be the mother?

"In the Bible book of the prophet Isaiah I found written that there is no God but the one true God. Idols and 'gods' are not the true Lord God, and therefore making sacrifices to them is pointless. For though they have eyes, they can't see; and though they have ears, they can't hear. I thought, if this is true, all the religion I've practised up until now is worthless. I decided that the Christian religion was unsuitable for Tibetans and stopped reading the Bible. Morning and evening in the hospital I went to worship with the Christians and acted as though I believed, but only because I felt obliged to them while they were taking care of me."

A Bhutanese girl named Sangey came to the hospital for treatment and began to live with Nyima. The Christians frowned on their actions, so Hyima left. Later however, he met an English Christian who encouraged him to start reading the Bible again. The two of them met daily to discuss Biblical themes. It proved a great struggle for Nyima. He had studied Buddhism for so many years, he just felt he couldn't leave it.

"The Christians were very devout, but I wondered why they made no offerings to their God. After all, it isn't a sin to make offerings, I thought. One day when I was reading the Bible's book of Isaiah, I found this: *'From one tree a man cuts a piece of wood, throws it in the fire and cooks his food. From another he makes an idol and bows down to it, praying to it: 'Save me!' But the idol doesn't answer and it cannot save'* (Isaiah 44:15ff). That simple but powerful verse greatly undermined by faith in the Buddhist gods."

Nyima took ill again. He contracted tuberculosis and found himself in a desperate state in hospital. A visiting Christian evangelist came and prayed for him to recover. Much to the amazement of his doctors Nyima did make a speedy recovery. This experience drove him all the more to his Bible. He read it in an earnest search for a final answer to all his questions. After thanking God for his recovery:

"I prayed and opened my Bible to the eleventh chapter of the book of Deuteronomy, the twenty-six and twenty-seventh verses: *'Today I have set before you a blessing and a curse – the blessing if you obey the commands of the Lord your God that I am giving you today; the curse if you disobey the commands of the Lord your God and turn from the way I command you today by following other gods, which you have not known.'* I searched further and read another very challenging and enlightening verse in the New Testament: *'If anyone sins, we have an Advocate in the presence of the Father – Jesus Christ, the Righteous One. He is the atoning sacrifice for our sins, and not only for ours but also for the sins of the whole world.'* (1 John 2:1). Turning to Ephesians 4:22-23 I read: *"With regard to your former way of life, put off your old self, which is being corrupted by deceitful desires, to be made new in the attitude of your minds: and to put on the new self, created to be like God in righteousness and holiness.'* The final place I looked was the tenth chapter of the book of Hebrews. Chapter 10:17-22 says: *'I will remember their sins and lawless acts no more. And where these have been forgiven there is no longer any sacrifice for sin…Let us draw near to God with a sincere heart in full assurance of faith, having our hearts sprinkled to cleanse us from a guilty conscience, and having our bodies washed with pure water'."*

It had taken three years of study but the word of God finally penetrated Nyima's heart. The Lord enabled him to turn away from his adultery, idolatry, drinking and, worst of all, his religious pride. He forsook it all and placed saving faith in the person and work of the Lord Jesus Christ. Now he was a real Christian! Before this, many people had urged him to be baptised, but he had always resisted because he was never really a Christian "on the inside"! In November 1955, a brother in Christ called Nathaniel baptised him at the Finnish Mission in Ghoom, near Darjeeling. He was the first Tibetan they had ever baptised.

Later, Nyima married another Tibetan from Lhasa, Rigdzin Wangmo. The two worked itrelessly for Jesus Christ, serving and helping the sick and suffering and telling all, including the Dalai Lama, about their Lord and Saviour. In May, 1972, Bishop Dindiel from Lucknow ordained Nyima as a pastor and he served in a church until 1982, and then in Nepal he worked amongst the Tibetan refugees until 1994.

CHAPTER 6

For the Reader

At an interfaith gathering at the Cathedral of St Patrick in New York in 1979, the Dalai Lama said, *"All the world's major religions are basically the same."* He was given a standing ovation. Afterwards a reporter asked a cardinal in attendance to give his opinion about the event. He responded: *"This is one of the dramatic movements of the Spirit in our time."* Globalism in religion is clearly keeping pace with globalism in politics.

While acknowledging superficial similarities between the world's major religions, one must also face the fact that the world's religions are, in truth, fundamentally different. They do not even share a belief in something as basic as one supreme Creator God. Hinduism teaches that: *"God is in truth the whole universe"* (Svetasvatara Upanishad 3). In Buddhism there is no need for a Creator. Buddhists today may be atheistic, agnostic or animistic. The Bible on the other hand explicitly states: *"In the beginning God created the heavens and the earth"* (Genesis 1:1).

In terms of a Creator, there are only really three options: either the universe is God, or the universe created itself, or God created it. If God *is* everything, then good and evil are part of God. The paedophile is as much an expression of God as the saint. What else are we to make of Krishna's words when he says, *"I am the source from which all creatures evolve…I am the sun…I am the moon…I am Prahlada, born among demons…I am death…I am the gambling of the gambler"* (Bhagavad Gita 10:8-36). Thus a Hindu may worship practically anything he wants and his gods may be sinners, just like himself. As for the theory that the universe created itself from nothing, surely there is little need to defend such a fantasy. From nothing, nothing comes. That leaves only one genuine option – God must have created the universe.

Most religions recognise the existence of both moral laws and an afterlife. Buddha taught, *"Do not what is evil. Do what is good. Keep your mind pure. This is the teaching of Buddha"* (Dhammapada 14:183). He also said, *"Those who do evil are reborn in hell; the righteous go to heaven"* (Dhammapada 9:126). However, only the Bible rules out the possibility of a person earning his or her way to heaven. It repeatedly declares that salvation is *"not by works, lest anyone should boast"* (Ephesians 2:8). In fact the Bible pronounces even our best efforts worthless: *"We are all like an unclean thing, and all our righteousnesses* [good deeds] *are like filthy rags"* (Isaiah 64:6). How so? Because when sin entered the world through our first parents' rebellion in the garden of Eden, their offspring were thereby marked and constituted sinners by nature (Romans 5:12-19). All human beings were thereafter born with a depraved principle of evil permeating their very inner being (Psalm 51:5, Ephesians 2:3, Isaiah 48:8, Psalm 58:3, John 3:6, Romans 7:18). Have you ever understood by the convicting power of the Spirit through God's Word, that you are, by nature, incurably bad, unfit for heaven and undeserving of grace and mercy, while the just wrath of a holy and righteous God hangs over your head? God cannot accept the good works of condemned sinners! The Bible asks: *"Who can say, 'I have made my heart clean, I am pure from my sin'?"* (Proverbs 20:9), and again: *"For there is not a just man on earth who does good and does not sin"* (Ecclesiastes 7:20).

Not even the founders of the great religions of the world can claim to be fit for heaven. Confucius said, *"As to being a Divine Sage or even a Good Man, far be it for me to make any such claim."*[1] Lao

Tze, the founder of Taoism stated, "*I alone appear empty. Ignorant am I, O so ignorant! I am dull! I alone am confused, so confused!*"[2] Guru Nanak, the founder of Sikhism wrote, "*I have become perplexed in my search. In darkness I find no way. Devoted to pride, I weep in sorrow. How shall deliverance be obtained?*"[3] Buddha, the founder of Buddhism admitted, "*Because in reality there are no living beings to whom the Lord Buddha can bring salvation.*"[4] Muhammad was advised, "*So be patient, [O Muhammad]. Indeed, the promise of Allah is truth. And ask forgiveness for your sin and exalt [Allah] with praise of your Lord in the evening and the morning.*"[5] The Prophet also said, "*O Allah! Set me apart from my sins (faults) as the East and West are set apart from each other and clean me from sins as a white garment is cleaned of dirt (after thorough washing). O Allah! Wash off my sins with water, snow and hail.*"[6] Even the gods of Hinduism in the *Siva Purana* are not immune from sin: "*All of you bands of gods are wicked.*"[7]

What a contrast to hear the words of Jesus Christ who challenged his hearers, "*Which of you convicts Me of sin?*" (John 8:46). He did no sin, He knew no sin and in Him is no sin (1 Peter 2:22, 2 Corinthians 5:21, 1 John 3:5). He is as bright sunshine in the midst of darkness. He lived a uniquely sinless life among sinful men. As the sinless Son of God, equal with God, He was the only one able to suffer and die for the sins of the world by becoming a sacrifice on the cross. Three days after His death He rose from the dead. This is perhaps the most striking difference of all between true Christianity and the rest of this world's religions. Consider the tombs of the world's religious leaders; they each contain the bones of dead men. Christ's tomb is empty. As the angel said, "*He is not here, He has risen.*" All of this after fulfilling scores of Biblical prophecies written about Him long before His birth. No one else comes close. Christ is unique.

So, why did he have to die on the cross and rise from the dead? Let's go back to the fact that all of us are sinners. That includes all religious leaders, and every priest and prophet. All of us are under God's condemnation because of sin. God views sin extremely seriously. If you die in your sins you will suffer under the God's judgment for ever in hell. That's what we all deserve. Yet God showed His amazing love and mercy by sending His Son to die on the cross, where He bore the wrath and judgment against sin, not His own.

The Bible summarises this wonderful plan of salvation in Romans 5:6-8, *"For when we were still without strength, in due time Christ died for the ungodly. For scarcely for a righteous man will one die; yet perhaps for a good man some would even dare to die. But God demonstrates His own love toward us, in that while we were still sinners, Christ died for us."*

In response to His grace, God calls on us to *"Repent and believe the gospel"* (Mark 1:15). This involves us abandoning all former and present trust in ourselves, our religion and our good works. It involves turning from sin and rejecting the lie of multifaithism and receiving the free gift of eternal life – that is, receiving the forgiveness of sins through trusting alone for salvation in the Lord Jesus Christ. He said, *"I am the Way, the Truth and the Life. No man comes to the Father except by Me"* (John 14:6). Today, if you will hear and obey His voice, harden not your heart.

---

1. Arthur Waley, trans., *The Analects of Confucius* (NY: Vintage, 1938), 130
2. *Tao-The-King,* 20:3, 20:5-7 cited in Robert E. Hume's *The World's Living Religions* (NY: Charles Scribner's Sons, 1959, rev.), 203
3. Hume, *The World's Living Religions,* 95
4. Robert O. Ballou, *The Portable World Bible: A Comprehensive Selection from the Eight Great Scriptures of the World,* (NY: Viking Press, 1968), 134, 147, 151
5. quranonline.net
6. *Hadith,* Vol. 1, Bk. 12, No. 711, narrated by Abu Huraim
7. From the *Siva Purana,* cited in *Hindu Myths,* (Penguin Classics, 1975), 164

If through this book you have trusted in the Lord Jesus Christ alone for your eternal salvation you should immediately take the following steps:

1. Thank Him for what He has done for you and ask yourself the question, "What can I now do for Him?"

2. Start speaking daily to Him in prayer from your heart, bringing Him praise and thanksgiving, as well as asking Him for blessings.

3. Obtain a Bible and start reading and studying it. It's best to begin with one of the Gospels (e.g. Mark or John). Then read through the New Testament, before progressing to the Old Testament. Ask God to give you understanding as to how to apply the Bible's teachings practically to your life.

4. Find a Bible believing Church and regularly attend its meetings and be baptised.

5. Tell others what the Lord Jesus has done for you.

Acknowledgements:
1. The publisher for *Destined for Royalty* is unknown.
2. *Holocaust* by kind permission of the publisher, Sean O'Sullivan, P.O. Box 7848, Johannesburg, South Africa, editor of the Good News Magazine.
3. Used by permission of Mark Gabriel, abridged from his book *Islam & Terrorism* (Charisma House, Lake Mary, Florida, 2002)
4. *From Tradition to Truth* by kind permission of the author.
5. *A Tibetan Monk's Story* by Nyima Chothar, published by Samdan Publishers, Post Box 2119, Kathmandu, Nepal, © Nima Tshering, KTM 1995

Also available:

Dawn of the New Age	*5 New Agers Relate Their Search for the Truth*
Angels of Light	*5 Spiritualists Test the Spirits*
The Pilgrimage	*5 Muslims Make the Greatest Discovery*
Witches and Wizards	*5 Witches Find Eternal Wisdom*
They Thought They Were Saved	*5 Christians Recall a Startling Discovery*
Messiah	*5 Jewish People Make the Greatest Discovery*
Light Seekers	*5 Hindus Search for God*
The Evolution Crisis	*5 Evolutionists Think Again*

If you would like confidential help or further information, please feel free to contact us. We can supply free Bibles, literature and details of Bible believing churches in your area. If this book has been a help to you please let us know. We greatly value the feedback we receive from our readers.

Published by:
John Ritchie Ltd.
40 Beansburn, Kilmarnock, Ayrshire, KA3 1RL.
Tel: +44 (0) 1563 536394
Fax: +44 (0) 1563 571191
Email: sales@johnritchie.co.uk
Web: www.ritchiechristianmedia.co.uk